Russell Stannard

The Lab Cats Switch On

A look at electricity and magnets

Illustrated by
Bill Ledger

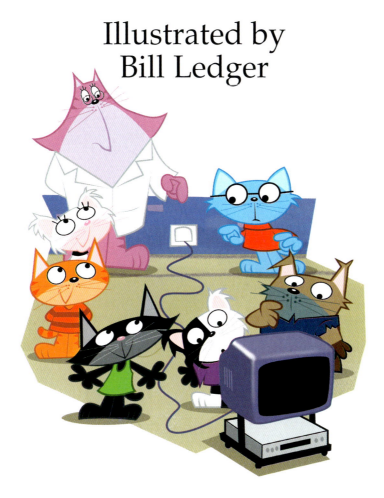

MARSHALL PUBLISHING • LONDON

Note to Parents

This **Lab Cats** book introduces magnetism and electricity to young children in an enjoyable way as they follow the adventures of a gang of cats. It can be read aloud while a younger child follows the words and pictures, or an older child can read it alone. Each experiment that the cats do is followed by the correct answers. Ask your child to give the answers before turning the page to see what the Lab Cats did. Any new or difficult scientific words are explained in "What the words mean" on page 36. Happy reading!

A Marshall Edition
Conceived, edited and designed by
Marshall Editions Ltd
The Orangery
161 New Bond Street
London W1S 2UF
www.marshallpublishing.com

First published in the UK in 2001 by
Marshall Publishing Ltd

10 9 8 7 6 5 4 3 2 1

Copyright © 2001 Marshall
Editions Developments Ltd
Text copyright © Russell Stannard
Illustrations copyright © Bill Ledger

All rights reserved. No part of this publication may be reproduced, stored in a retrieval system, or transmitted, in any form or by any means, electronic, mechanical, photocopying, recording or otherwise, without prior written permission from the publisher.

ISBN 1 8 4028 556 7

Originated in the UK by Hilo
Printed in Portugal by Printer Portuguesa

Editor: Rosalind Beckman
Managing Designer: Caroline Sangster
Art Director: Simon Webb
Editorial Manager: Janet Sacks
US Consultant: Dr Roberta Butler
Production: Christina Schuster

At night, when the children had gone home from school, it was the turn of the neighbourhood cats to have lessons. Their teacher was the caretaker's cat, the Prof.

"Good evening, Lab Cats," she greeted them.

"Good evening, Prof," they replied.

"Are we all here?" she asked. They called out their names.

"Today the children learnt about magnets," she said.

"Magnets come in different shapes," the Prof said. "But they all have two ends, called *poles*. One end is called the north pole, and the other end the south pole.

"The red end of each magnet is the north pole. See what happens when you bring two magnets up close to each other."

Swot wrote down what they discovered in his notebook. "When you try to bring both the north poles or the south poles of two magnets together, they push each other away. They *repel* each other. But when you bring the north pole of one magnet close to the south pole of another, they pull towards each other. They *attract* each other."

Are there any magnets in your home?

"There are lots of pretty magnets stuck all over this fridge door," remarked Precious.

"Yes," said the Prof. "Magnets can attract other things besides magnets. They attract anything made of iron or steel – like the fridge door.

"Take a look at these objects. Guess which of them a magnet will attract, and which it won't."

"You can then experiment with a magnet to find out if you were right," the Prof continued. "You can show your results in a table by putting a tick for each object in the correct column."

"Hey!" cried Basher. "Some of these drink cans are magnetic and some aren't."

"That's right," said the Prof. "You can only find out by testing the cans. Not all metals are magnetic. Aluminium, brass and copper are not…"

"Cop-purr, did you say?" Lucky purred, happily.

"My magnet's not much good," complained Fluff. "It hardly picks up anything – just one paper clip."

"There are strong magnets and weak magnets. Yours is a weak one," explained the Prof. "Who can tell me how we could test the strength of a magnet? Fluff's pile of paper clips gives you a clue."

Can you think of a way to test the strength of a magnet?

"I know, I know!" cried Swot, excitedly. "We could see how many paper clips magnets of different sizes will pick up," he said.

"Exactly," agreed the Prof. "You will then be able to find out the strength of each magnet."

My magnet has picked up six.

And mine has picked up eight.

"I've got an idea, too," said Precious. "Look! We can see how fast the magnets make this little boat cross to the other side of the fish tank."

"Excellent!" exclaimed the Prof. "That's another way of measuring a magnetic force."

"It's funny how this magnetic force reaches across space," said Fluff. "You can feel it even though the magnets aren't touching. I wonder if it reaches out through water."

"Let's try it, shall we?" said the Prof.

They scattered some paper clips over the floor of the fish tank, and held a magnet close to its side.

"Look!" exclaimed Fluff, excitedly. "The magnet is pulling the paper clips through the water."

"What else does a magnet work through?" asked the Prof.

"How do you make magnets?" asked Ginger.

"I'll show you," replied the Prof. "First you need something made of steel."

She found a large, blunt needle and began stroking it with the end of a magnet. She did this several times.

"The needle is now a magnet," she announced.

Always stroke the needle in the same direction.

Try making a steel screwdriver magnetic by stroking it with a fridge magnet.

"Really!?" exclaimed Ginger. Sure enough, he found that the needle could now pick up a paper clip.

"How long will it stay magnetic?" asked Lucky.

"Quite a long time," replied the Prof. "Test it tomorrow and see. But now I want to show you how you can use the magnetic needle to make a compass."

"What's a compass?" asked Ginger.

"A compass always points north. When you are out, a compass helps you to find the direction you want. We can make a compass by taping a small wooden stick – this used match will do nicely – to a magnetised needle."

When they had made the compass, they floated it on the water. The needle twisted round.

Watch the compass find the right direction.

It's turning round!

"There!" said the Prof. "When the needle is magnetic and free to move, it always points to the north."

The Lab Cats were amazed.

"Try turning the needle to face other ways," the Prof suggested.

They did as she said. To their delight, they discovered the needle always came back to point north.

"You can't see the magnetic force," declared Fluff.
"It's invisible – just like gravity," said Precious.
"Are there any more invisible forces, Prof?" asked Swot.
"Yes," the Prof replied. "There is an electric force."
"What's that?" asked Basher.

"The electric force makes your fur stand on end when it is brushed. It lets you pick up bits of paper with a comb if it has been rubbed. It attracts a hanky to the screen of a TV set that is on."

"But where does the force come from?" Basher insisted.

"When Lucky rubs the ballooon against her sweater, both become electrically charged," explained the Prof.

"If the electric charge is unable to flow through the material, it stays on the surface as static electricity. The electric charge on the balloon and the sweater then pull towards each other."

That's a good party trick.

Hey! The balloon is sticking to me.

"But what's that to do with electricity?" asked Basher. "When an electric charge can move from one place to another, we get an electric current," replied the Prof. "Currents can pass through certain materials such as metals and water. We call these materials *conductors*. But there are other materials that currents can't pass through, such as rubber, plastic, or glass. These we call *insulators*."

"I know," said Fluff. "The rubber ball and wooden spoon are insulators, and the key and coins are conductors."

"Good!" said the Prof. "And where do you think electricity comes from?"

"From that socket in the wall over there," replied Precious. "And from batteries that you buy in the shops."

"That's right," said the Prof. "So, which of these things here need electricity to work?"

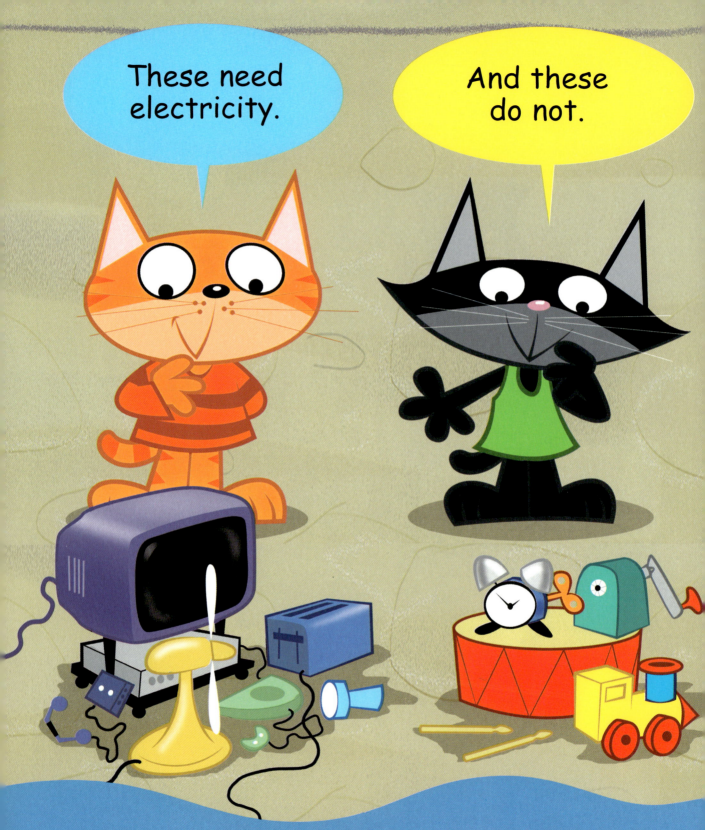

"Electricity can be used to make sound or light," said the Prof. "It can get things moving. It can also be used to give out heat. What do these things do?"

"Now, in order to use electricity, you need to have a circuit," said Prof.

"What's that?" asked Fluff.

"Well, this battery has two terminals made of metal. The electricity comes out of the battery from one terminal, then goes back to the battery through the other. But it can only do that if we make a circuit, or path, for it to travel round."

"A kind of race track for electricity?" suggested Lucky. The Prof smiled and nodded. "To make this bell work, we have to get the electricity to the bell from the battery."

"And then the electricity has to get back to the battery again from the bell," said Lucky.

"We can make a circuit by connecting the bell to the battery with wires," said the Prof. "We use metal wires because they conduct electricity."

I'm going to connect this to the other terminal.

"Of course, lights, bells, or electric fires do not need to be on all the time," said the Prof. "So most circuits have a switch in them. When the switch is *on*, the circuit is complete and the electricity flows. When the switch is *off*, it opens up a gap in the circuit and the electricity stops."

"Often we need more powerful electricity than we can get from a battery," she continued. "This electricity comes from a power station. It travels along wires and through sockets in the wall. This electricity can be dangerous, so we have to be extra careful with it."

"Excellent!" exclaimed the Prof. "You're being very sensible. But now it's time for you to be going."

"Not already!" the Lab Cats cried in disappointment.

"I'm afraid so. Hurry up please. I have to switch off the lights."

Off you go, Lab Cats! Good night!

What the words mean

Battery It produces an electric current.

Circuit A closed path which connects one terminal of a source of electricity, such as a battery, to the other.

Compass A magnet that is used to tell which direction is north.

Conductor Any material through which an electric current can pass.

Electric charge When certain materials rub against one another, they each gain an electric charge.

Electric current A flow of electric charge in a conductor.

Electric force The force with which electric charges pull on each other.

Insulator Any material that does not allow an electric current to pass through it.

Magnets Materials that attract certain metals. They attract or repel other magnets.

Magnetic force The force produced by magnets.

Poles Magnets have two ends called poles: the north (N) pole, and the south (S) pole. Two N or two S poles repel each other; a N pole and a S pole attract each other.

Static electricity Electric charge that is not moving.

Switch Something that can cause a break in a circuit and stop the flow of a current.

Terminals The two metal parts of a battery through which the current flows in and out. Wires are fastened to the terminals to make a circuit.